Gifts in a Jar create no-fuss, homemade treats your family and friends will love. Simply layer the ingredients in a 1-quart container of your choice. Be creative in selecting the perfect jar or glass canister for your gift! The most common container used for Gifts in a Jar are wide-mouth 1-quart canning jars.

• To keep mess to a minimum, shape a flexible paper plate into a funnel. Use the homemade funnel when adding each layer.

• Be sure to pack down each ingredient before adding the next.

• Lightly tap the jar on the countertop after adding ingredients like flour and powdered sugar to ensure there are no air bubbles.

• If you wish to cover your jar lid with fabric, you will need a 7 to 8″ fabric circle. Then use a rubber band to hold the fabric in place before attaching the tag with ribbon or raffia.

• Don't forget to personalize each gift tag before attaching it to the jar.

• Make several Gifts in a Jar and include them as part of a gift basket. Personalize each basket according to the occasion or recipient. A large mixing bowl filled with Gifts in a Jar, kitchen towels, pot holders and utensils makes a great gift.

• Each gift should keep up to six months. If the mix contains nuts, it should be used within three months.

Printed in the United States of America
by G&R Publishing Co.

Published By:

507 Industrial Street
Waverly, IA 50677

ISBN-13: 978-1-56383-306-9
ISBN-10: 1-56383-306-9
Item #3011

Reese's Monster Cookie Mix

½ C. chopped unsalted peanuts
½ C. Reese's Pieces candy
½ C. milk chocolate chips
1½ C. all-purpose flour
1 T. baking soda
½ T. baking powder
¼ tsp. salt
½ C. dark brown sugar
¾ C. sugar

In a 1-quart container of your choice, layer the above ingredients in order given. Pack each layer into the container before adding the next ingredient.

Securely close container and, if desired, decorate with fabric, ribbon or raffia. Cut out a gift tag with the recipient's directions from the following pages. Simply personalize the tag and attach to your container.

Reese's Monster Cookies

1 jar Reese's Monster Cookie Mix
½ C. butter or margarine, softened
1 egg
⅓ C. creamy or crunchy peanut butter
½ tsp. vanilla

Preheat oven to 375°. In a large mixing bowl, pour sugar and brown sugar from top of jar. Add butter and mix at high speed until light in texture. Add egg, peanut butter and vanilla and beat at high speed for 1 to 2 minutes. Add remaining ingredients from jar and beat at low speed until well combined. Drop dough by tablespoonfuls onto a lightly greased baking sheet. Bake for 10 to 12 minutes.

Reese's Monster Cookies

1 jar Reese's Monster Cookie Mix
½ C. butter or margarine, softened
1 egg
⅓ C. creamy or crunchy peanut butter
½ tsp. vanilla

Preheat oven to 375°. In a large mixing bowl, pour sugar and brown sugar from top of jar. Add butter and mix at high speed until light in texture. Add egg, peanut butter and vanilla and beat at high speed for 1 to 2 minutes. Add remaining ingredients from jar and beat at low speed until well combined. Drop dough by tablespoonfuls onto a lightly greased baking sheet. Bake for 10 to 12 minutes.

For a quality black and white reproduction, photocopy the above tag. Any of the color tags may also be photocopied for additional gifts.

Reese's Monster Cookies

1 jar Reese's Monster
Cookie Mix
½ C. butter or margarine,
softened
1 egg
⅓ C. creamy or crunchy
peanut butter
½ tsp. vanilla

Preheat oven to 375°. In a large mixing bowl, pour sugar and brown sugar from top of jar. Add butter and mix at high speed until light in texture. Add egg, peanut butter and vanilla and beat at high speed for 1 to 2 minutes. Add remaining ingredients from jar and beat at low speed until well combined. Drop dough by tablespoonfuls onto a lightly greased baking sheet. Bake for 10 to 12 minutes.

Reese's Monster Cookies

1 jar Reese's Monster
Cookie Mix
½ C. butter or margarine,
softened
1 egg
⅓ C. creamy or
crunchy peanut butter
½ tsp. vanilla

Preheat oven to 375°. In a large mixing bowl, pour sugar and brown sugar from top of jar. Add butter and mix at high speed until light in texture. Add egg, peanut butter and vanilla and beat at high speed for 1 to 2 minutes. Add remaining ingredients from jar and beat at low speed until well combined. Drop dough by tablespoonfuls onto a lightly greased baking sheet. Bake for 10 to 12 minutes.

Reese's Monster Cookies

1 jar Reese's Monster
Cookie Mix
½ C. butter or margarine,
softened
1 egg
⅓ C. creamy or crunchy
peanut butter
½ tsp. vanilla

Preheat oven to 375°. In a large mixing bowl, pour sugar and brown sugar from top of jar. Add butter and mix at high speed until light in texture. Add egg, peanut butter and vanilla and beat at high speed for 1 to 2 minutes. Add remaining ingredients from jar and beat at low speed until well combined. Drop dough by tablespoonfuls onto a lightly greased baking sheet. Bake for 10 to 12 minutes.

Reese's Monster Cookies

1 jar Reese's Monster
Cookie Mix
½ C. butter or margarine,
softened
1 egg
⅓ C. creamy or crunchy
peanut butter
½ tsp. vanilla

Preheat oven to 375°. In a large mixing bowl, pour sugar and brown sugar from top of jar. Add butter and mix at high speed until light in texture. Add egg, peanut butter and vanilla and beat at high speed for 1 to 2 minutes. Add remaining ingredients from jar and beat at low speed until well combined. Drop dough by tablespoonfuls onto a lightly greased baking sheet. Bake for 10 to 12 minutes.

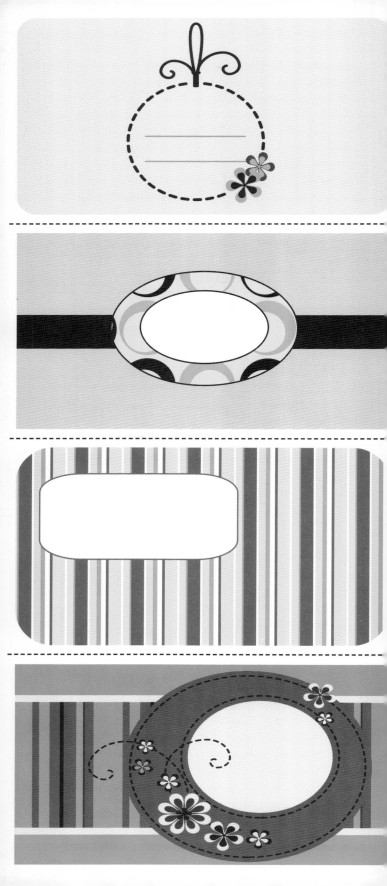

Friendship Brownie Mix

⅔ C. sugar
½ C. white baking chips
½ C. semi-sweet chocolate chips
½ C. walnuts
⅔ C. brown sugar
⅓ C. unsweetened cocoa powder
1 C. all-purpose flour
1 tsp. baking soda
½ tsp. salt

Layer the ingredients in the order given into a
1-quart container of your choice. After adding
the unsweetened cocoa powder, but before
adding the flour, clean the inside of the jar with
a paper towel. Pack each layer into the container
before adding the next ingredient.

Securely close container and, if desired, decorate
with fabric, ribbon or raffia. Cut out a gift
tag with the recipient's directions from the
following pages. Simply personalize the tag
and attach to your container.

Friendship Brownies

3 eggs
⅔ C. vegetable oil
1 tsp. vanilla
1 jar Friendship Brownie Mix

Preheat oven to 350°. In a large bowl, mix the eggs, oil and vanilla. Add the Friendship Brownie Mix. Stir until the mixture is well-blended. Spread in a greased 9″ square baking pan. Bake for 34 to 38 minutes or until a toothpick inserted in the center comes out clean. Cool before cutting.

Friendship Brownies

3 eggs
⅔ C. vegetable oil
1 tsp. vanilla
1 jar Friendship Brownie Mix

Preheat oven to 350°. In a large bowl, mix the eggs, oil and vanilla. Add the Friendship Brownie Mix. Stir until the mixture is well-blended. Spread in a greased 9″ square baking pan. Bake for 34 to 38 minutes or until a toothpick inserted in the center comes out clean. Cool before cutting.

For a quality black and white reproduction, photocopy the above tag.
Any of the color tags may also be photocopied for additional gifts.

Friendship Brownies

3 eggs
⅔ C. vegetable oil
1 tsp. vanilla
1 jar Friendship
  Brownie Mix

Preheat oven to 350°. In a large bowl, mix the eggs, oil and vanilla. Add the Friendship Brownie Mix. Stir until the mixture is well-blended. Spread in a greased 9″ square baking pan. Bake for 34 to 38 minutes or until a toothpick inserted in the center comes out clean. Cool before cutting.

Friendship Brownies

3 eggs
⅔ C. vegetable oil
1 tsp. vanilla
1 jar Friendship
  Brownie Mix

Preheat oven to 350°. In a large bowl, mix the eggs, oil and vanilla. Add the Friendship Brownie Mix. Stir until the mixture is well-blended. Spread in a greased 9″ square baking pan. Bake for 34 to 38 minutes or until a toothpick inserted in the center comes out clean. Cool before cutting.

Friendship Brownies

3 eggs
⅔ C. vegetable oil
1 tsp. vanilla
1 jar Friendship
  Brownie Mix

Preheat oven to 350°. In a large bowl, mix the eggs, oil and vanilla. Add the Friendship Brownie Mix. Stir until the mixture is well-blended. Spread in a greased 9″ square baking pan. Bake for 34 to 38 minutes or until a toothpick inserted in the center comes out clean. Cool before cutting.

Friendship Brownies

3 eggs
⅔ C. vegetable oil
1 tsp. vanilla
1 jar Friendship
  Brownie Mix

Preheat oven to 350°. In a large bowl, mix the eggs, oil and vanilla. Add the Friendship Brownie Mix. Stir until the mixture is well-blended. Spread in a greased 9″ square baking pan. Bake for 34 to 38 minutes or until a toothpick inserted in the center comes out clean. Cool before cutting.

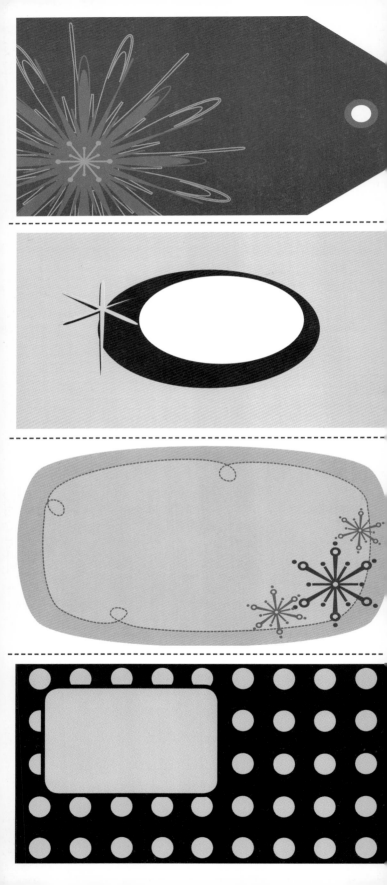

Triple Chocolate Chip Cookie Mix

½ C. milk chocolate chips
½ C. white chocolate chips
½ C. semi-sweet chocolate chips
1¼ C. all-purpose flour
1 tsp. baking soda
Pinch of salt
½ C. unsweetened cocoa powder
¾ C. sugar

In a 1-quart container of your choice, layer the above ingredients in order given. Pack each layer into the container before adding the next ingredient.

Securely close container and, if desired, decorate with fabric, ribbon or raffia. Cut out a gift tag with the recipient's directions from the following pages. Simply personalize the tag and attach to your container.

Triple Chocolate Chip Cookies

¾ C. butter or margarine, softened
1 jar Triple Chocolate Chip Cookie Mix
1 egg
1 tsp. vanilla

Preheat oven to 375°. In a large mixing bowl, cream butter until light in texture. Pour sugar from the top of jar and beat with butter on high speed until light and fluffy. Add egg and vanilla and beat at medium speed until well combined. Add remaining ingredients from jar and mix at medium speed until combined. Drop dough by teaspoonfuls onto a lightly greased baking sheet. Bake for 10 to 12 minutes.

Triple Chocolate Chip Cookies

¾ C. butter or margarine, softened
1 jar Triple Chocolate Chip Cookie Mix
1 egg
1 tsp. vanilla

Preheat oven to 375°. In a large mixing bowl, cream butter until light in texture. Pour sugar from the top of jar and beat with butter on high speed until light and fluffy. Add egg and vanilla and beat at medium speed until well combined. Add remaining ingredients from jar and mix at medium speed until combined. Drop dough by teaspoonfuls onto a lightly greased baking sheet. Bake for 10 to 12 minutes.

For a quality black and white reproduction, photocopy the above tag. Any of the color tags may also be photocopied for additional gifts.

Triple Chocolate Chip Cookies

¾ C. butter or margarine, softened

1 jar Triple Chocolate Chip Cookie Mix

1 egg

1 tsp. vanilla

Preheat oven to 375°. In a large mixing bowl, cream butter until light in texture. Pour sugar from the top of jar and beat with butter on high speed until light and fluffy. Add egg and vanilla and beat at medium speed until well combined. Add remaining ingredients from jar and mix at medium speed until combined. Drop dough by teaspoonfuls onto a lightly greased baking sheet. Bake for 10 to 12 minutes.

Triple Chocolate Chip Cookies

¾ C. butter or margarine, softened

1 jar Triple Chocolate Chip Cookie Mix

1 egg

1 tsp. vanilla

Preheat oven to 375°. In a large mixing bowl, cream butter until light in texture. Pour sugar from the top of jar and beat with butter on high speed until light and fluffy. Add egg and vanilla and beat at medium speed until well combined. Add remaining ingredients from jar and mix at medium speed until combined. Drop dough by teaspoonfuls onto a lightly greased baking sheet. Bake for 10 to 12 minutes.

Triple Chocolate Chip Cookies

¾ C. butter or margarine, softened

1 jar Triple Chocolate Chip Cookie Mix

1 egg

1 tsp. vanilla

Preheat oven to 375°. In a large mixing bowl, cream butter until light in texture. Pour sugar from the top of jar and beat with butter on high speed until light and fluffy. Add egg and vanilla and beat at medium speed until well combined. Add remaining ingredients from jar and mix at medium speed until combined. Drop dough by teaspoonfuls onto a lightly greased baking sheet. Bake for 10 to 12 minutes.

Triple Chocolate Chip Cookies

¾ C. butter or margarine, softened

1 jar Triple Chocolate Chip Cookie Mix

1 egg

1 tsp. vanilla

Preheat oven to 375°. In a large mixing bowl, cream butter until light in texture. Pour sugar from the top of jar and beat with butter on high speed until light and fluffy. Add egg and vanilla and beat at medium speed until well combined. Add remaining ingredients from jar and mix at medium speed until combined. Drop dough by teaspoonfuls onto a lightly greased baking sheet. Bake for 10 to 12 minutes.

Cookies n' Cream Chocolate Chip Cake Mix

1 C. sugar
2 C. all-purpose flour
½ C. mini chocolate chips
¾ C. crushed Oreo cookies
1 T. baking powder
½ tsp. salt

In a 1-quart container of your choice, layer the above ingredients in order given. Pack each layer into the container before adding the next ingredient.

Securely close container and, if desired, decorate with fabric, ribbon or raffia. Cut out a gift tag with the recipient's directions from the following pages. Simply personalize the tag and attach to your container.

Cookies n' Cream Chocolate Chip Cake

1 jar Cookies n' Cream Chocolate
    Chip Cake Mix
½ C. butter or margarine
1 C. milk
2 tsp. vanilla
3 egg whites
Vanilla frosting

Preheat oven to 350°. In a large mixing bowl, add the contents of jar. Cut in butter with a pastry blender. Add milk, vanilla and egg whites and beat at low speed for 30 seconds. Scrape sides of bowl and beat at medium speed for 2 minutes. Pour cake batter into a lightly greased and floured 9 x 13″ baking dish. Bake for 30 to 35 minutes. Frost cake with vanilla frosting.

Cookies n' Cream Chocolate Chip Cake

1 jar Cookies n' Cream
    Chocolate Chip Cake Mix
½ C. butter or margarine
1 C. milk
2 tsp. vanilla
    3 egg whites
    Vanilla frosting

Preheat oven to 350°. In a large mixing bowl, add the contents of jar. Cut in butter with a pastry blender. Add milk, vanilla and egg whites and beat at low speed for 30 seconds. Scrape sides of bowl and beat at medium speed for 2 minutes. Pour cake batter into a lightly greased and floured 9 x 13″ baking dish. Bake for 30 to 35 minutes. Frost cake with vanilla frosting.

For a quality black and white reproduction, photocopy the above tag.
Any of the color tags may also be photocopied for additional gifts.

Cookies n' Cream Chocolate Chip Cake

1 jar Cookies n' Cream
   Chocolate Chip Cake Mix
½ C. butter or margarine
1 C. milk
2 tsp. vanilla
3 egg whites
Vanilla frosting

Preheat oven to 350°. In a large mixing bowl, add the contents of jar. Cut in butter with a pastry blender. Add milk, vanilla and egg whites and beat at low speed for 30 seconds. Scrape sides of bowl and beat at medium speed for 2 minutes. Pour cake batter into a lightly greased and floured 9 x 13″ baking dish. Bake for 30 to 35 minutes. Frost cake with vanilla frosting.

Cookies n' Cream Chocolate Chip Cake

1 jar Cookies n' Cream
   Chocolate Chip Cake Mix
½ C. butter or margarine
1 C. milk
2 tsp. vanilla
3 egg whites
Vanilla frosting

Preheat oven to 350°. In a large mixing bowl, add the contents of jar. Cut in butter with a pastry blender. Add milk, vanilla and egg whites and beat at low speed for 30 seconds. Scrape sides of bowl and beat at medium speed for 2 minutes. Pour cake batter into a lightly greased and floured 9 x 13″ baking dish. Bake for 30 to 35 minutes. Frost cake with vanilla frosting.

Cookies n' Cream Chocolate Chip Cake

1 jar Cookies n' Cream
   Chocolate Chip Cake Mix
½ C. butter or margarine
1 C. milk
2 tsp. vanilla
3 egg whites
Vanilla frosting

Preheat oven to 350°. In a large mixing bowl, add the contents of jar. Cut in butter with a pastry blender. Add milk, vanilla and egg whites and beat at low speed for 30 seconds. Scrape sides of bowl and beat at medium speed for 2 minutes. Pour cake batter into a lightly greased and floured 9 x 13″ baking dish. Bake for 30 to 35 minutes. Frost cake with vanilla frosting.

Cookies n' Cream Chocolate Chip Cake

1 jar Cookies n' Cream
   Chocolate Chip Cake
   Mix
½ C. butter or margarine
1 C. milk
2 tsp. vanilla
3 egg whites
Vanilla frosting

Preheat oven to 350°. In a large mixing bowl, add the contents of jar. Cut in butter with a pastry blender. Add milk, vanilla and egg whites and beat at low speed for 30 seconds. Scrape sides of bowl and beat at medium speed for 2 minutes. Pour cake batter into a lightly greased and floured 9 x 13″ baking dish. Bake for 30 to 35 minutes. Frost cake with vanilla frosting.

Chocolate Chip Muffin Mix

½ C. milk chocolate chips
⅔ C. brown sugar
⅛ tsp. salt
1½ tsp. baking powder
½ tsp. baking soda
1 tsp. ground cinnamon
½ tsp. ground nutmeg
2 C. all-purpose flour

In a 1-quart container of your choice, layer the above ingredients in order given. Pack each layer into the container before adding the next ingredient.

Securely close container and, if desired, decorate with fabric, ribbon or raffia. Cut out a gift tag with the recipient's directions from the following pages. Simply personalize the tag and attach to your container.

Chocolate Chip Muffins

1 jar Chocolate Chip Muffin Mix
¾ C. buttermilk
¾ C. applesauce
1 egg, slightly beaten
1½ T. vegetable oil
1 tsp. vanilla

Preheat oven to 350°. In a large bowl, combine the Chocolate Chip Muffin Mix with the buttermilk, applesauce, egg, oil and vanilla. Stir until the mixture is just blended. Do not over-mix. Spoon the batter into greased muffin tins, filling ⅔ to ¾ full. Bake for 18 to 20 minutes, or until golden brown. Cool on a wire rack for 10 minutes before removing. Serve warm or at room temperature.

Chocolate Chip Muffins

1 jar Chocolate Chip Muffin Mix
¾ C. buttermilk
¾ C. applesauce
1 egg, slightly beaten
1½ T. vegetable oil
1 tsp. vanilla

Preheat oven to 350°. In a large bowl, combine the Chocolate Chip Muffin Mix with the buttermilk, applesauce, egg, oil and vanilla. Stir until the mixture is just blended. Do not over-mix. Spoon the batter into greased muffin tins, filling ⅔ to ¾ full. Bake for 18 to 20 minutes, or until golden brown. Cool on a wire rack for 10 minutes before removing. Serve warm, or at room temperature.

For a quality black and white reproduction, photocopy the above tag.
Any of the color tags may also be photocopied for additional gifts.

Chocolate Chip Muffins

1 jar Chocolate Chip
  Muffin Mix
¾ C. buttermilk
¾ C. applesauce
1 egg, slightly beaten
1½ T. vegetable oil
1 tsp. vanilla

Preheat oven to 350°. In a large bowl, combine the Chocolate Chip Muffin Mix with the buttermilk, applesauce, egg, oil and vanilla. Stir until the mixture is just blended. Do not over-mix. Spoon the batter into greased muffin tins, filling ⅔ to ¾ full. Bake for 18 to 20 minutes, or until golden brown. Cool on a wire rack for 10 minutes before removing. Serve warm, or at room temperature.

Chocolate Chip Muffins

1 jar Chocolate Chip
  Muffin Mix
¾ C. buttermilk
¾ C. applesauce
1 egg, slightly beaten
1½ T. vegetable oil
1 tsp. vanilla

Preheat oven to 350°. In a large bowl, combine the Chocolate Chip Muffin Mix with the buttermilk, applesauce, egg, oil and vanilla. Stir until the mixture is just blended. Do not over-mix. Spoon the batter into greased muffin tins, filling ⅔ to ¾ full. Bake for 18 to 20 minutes, or until golden brown. Cool on a wire rack for 10 minutes before removing. Serve warm, or at room temperature.

Chocolate Chip Muffins

1 jar Chocolate Chip
  Muffin Mix
¾ C. buttermilk
¾ C. applesauce
1 egg, slightly beaten
1½ T. vegetable oil
1 tsp. vanilla

Preheat oven to 350°. In a large bowl, combine the Chocolate Chip Muffin Mix with the buttermilk, applesauce, egg, oil and vanilla. Stir until the mixture is just blended. Do not over-mix. Spoon the batter into greased muffin tins, filling ⅔ to ¾ full. Bake for 18 to 20 minutes, or until golden brown. Cool on a wire rack for 10 minutes before removing. Serve warm, or at room temperature.

Chocolate Chip Muffins

1 jar Chocolate Chip
  Muffin Mix
¾ C. buttermilk
¾ C. applesauce
1 egg, slightly beaten
1½ T. vegetable oil
1 tsp. vanilla

Preheat oven to 350°. In a large bowl, combine the Chocolate Chip Muffin Mix with the buttermilk, applesauce, egg, oil and vanilla. Stir until the mixture is just blended. Do not over-mix. Spoon the batter into greased muffin tins, filling ⅔ to ¾ full. Bake for 18 to 20 minutes, or until golden brown. Cool on a wire rack for 10 minutes before removing. Serve warm, or at room temperature.

Sour Cream Spice Cake Mix

¾ C. all-purpose flour
½ C. finely chopped walnuts
¾ C. raisins
1¼ C. brown sugar
1 C. all-purpose flour
2 tsp. ground cinnamon
¾ tsp. ground cloves
½ tsp. ground nutmeg
1¼ tsp. baking soda
1 tsp. baking powder
½ tsp. salt

In a 1-quart container of your choice, layer the above ingredients in order given. Pack each layer into the container before adding the next ingredient.

Securely close container and, if desired, decorate with fabric, ribbon or raffia. Cut out a gift tag with the recipient's directions from the following pages. Simply personalize the tag and attach to your container.

Sour Cream Spice Cake

1 jar Sour Cream Spice Cake Mix
¼ C. butter or margarine
¼ C. shortening
½ C. water
1 C. sour cream
2 eggs

Preheat oven to 350°. In a large bowl, empty contents of jar. Cut in butter and shortening using a pastry blender. Add water, sour cream and eggs and beat at low speed for 30 seconds. Scrape sides of bowl and beat at medium speed for 2 minutes. Pour batter into a lightly greased and floured 9 x 13″ baking dish. Bake for 40 to 45 minutes.

Sour Cream Spice Cake

1 jar Sour Cream
   Spice Cake Mix
¼ C. butter or
   margarine
¼ C. shortening
½ C. water
1 C. sour cream
 2 eggs

Preheat oven to 350°. In a large bowl, empty contents of jar. Cut in butter and shortening using a pastry blender. Add water, sour cream and eggs and beat at low speed for 30 seconds. Scrape sides of bowl and beat at medium speed for 2 minutes. Pour batter into a lightly greased and floured 9 x 13″ baking dish. Bake for 40 to 45 minutes.

For a quality black and white reproduction, photocopy the above tag. Any of the color tags may also be photocopied for additional gifts.

Sour Cream Spice Cake

1 jar Sour Cream Spice Cake Mix
¼ C. butter or margarine
¼ C. shortening
½ C. water
1 C. sour cream
2 eggs

Preheat oven to 350°. In a large bowl, empty contents of jar. Cut in butter and shortening using a pastry blender. Add water, sour cream and eggs and beat at low speed for 30 seconds. Scrape sides of bowl and beat at medium speed for 2 minutes. Pour batter into a lightly greased and floured 9 x 13″ baking dish. Bake for 40 to 45 minutes.

Sour Cream Spice Cake

1 jar Sour Cream Spice Cake Mix
¼ C. butter or margarine
¼ C. shortening
½ C. water
1 C. sour cream
2 eggs

Preheat oven to 350°. In a large bowl, empty contents of jar. Cut in butter and shortening using a pastry blender. Add water, sour cream and eggs and beat at low speed for 30 seconds. Scrape sides of bowl and beat at medium speed for 2 minutes. Pour batter into a lightly greased and floured 9 x 13″ baking dish. Bake for 40 to 45 minutes.

Sour Cream Spice Cake

1 jar Sour Cream Spice Cake Mix
¼ C. butter or margarine
¼ C. shortening
½ C. water
1 C. sour cream
2 eggs

Preheat oven to 350°. In a large bowl, empty contents of jar. Cut in butter and shortening using a pastry blender. Add water, sour cream and eggs and beat at low speed for 30 seconds. Scrape sides of bowl and beat at medium speed for 2 minutes. Pour batter into a lightly greased and floured 9 x 13″ baking dish. Bake for 40 to 45 minutes.

Sour Cream Spice Cake

1 jar Sour Cream Spice Cake Mix
¼ C. butter or margarine
¼ C. shortening
½ C. water
1 C. sour cream
2 eggs

Preheat oven to 350°. In a large bowl, empty contents of jar. Cut in butter and shortening using a pastry blender. Add water, sour cream and eggs and beat at low speed for 30 seconds. Scrape sides of bowl and beat at medium speed for 2 minutes. Pour batter into a lightly greased and floured 9 x 13″ baking dish. Bake for 40 to 45 minutes.

Coconut Macadamia Cookie Mix

½ C. chopped macadamia nuts
¾ C. shredded coconut, lightly toasted*
¾ C. sugar
1 tsp. baking soda
1¾ C. all-purpose flour
½ C. dark brown sugar

* To toast, spread shredded coconut out in a single layer on a baking sheet. Bake in oven at 350° until light golden brown, approximately 8 to 10 minutes. Cool completely before adding to jar.

In a 1-quart container of your choice, layer the above ingredients in order given. Pack each layer into the container before adding the next ingredient.

Securely close container and, if desired, decorate with fabric, ribbon or raffia. Cut out a gift tag with the recipient's directions from the following pages. Simply personalize the tag and attach to your container.

Coconut Macadamia Cookies

1 jar Coconut Macadamia Cookie Mix
¾ C. butter or margarine, softened
1 egg

Preheat oven to 375°. In a large mixing bowl, pour brown sugar from top of jar. Add butter and mix at high speed until light in texture. Add egg and remaining contents of jar and beat at low speed until well combined. Drop dough by teaspoonfuls onto a lightly greased baking sheet. Bake for 8 to 10 minutes.

Coconut Macadamia Cookies

1 jar Coconut Macadamia Cookie Mix
¾ C. butter or margarine, softened
1 egg

Preheat oven to 375°. In a large mixing bowl, pour brown sugar from top of jar. Add butter and mix at high speed until light in texture. Add egg and remaining contents of jar and beat at low speed until well combined. Drop dough by teaspoonfuls onto a lightly greased baking sheet. Bake for 8 to 10 minutes.

For a quality black and white reproduction, photocopy the above tag. Any of the color tags may also be photocopied for additional gifts.

Coconut Macadamia Cookies

1 jar Coconut Macadamia
Cookie Mix

¾ C. butter or margarine,
softened

1 egg

Preheat oven to 375°. In a large mixing bowl, pour brown sugar from top of jar. Add butter and mix at high speed until lightened in texture. Add egg and remaining contents of jar and beat at low speed until well combined. Drop dough by teaspoonfuls onto a lightly greased baking sheet. Bake for 8 to 10 minutes.

Coconut Macadamia Cookies

1 jar Coconut Macadamia
Cookie Mix

¾ C. butter or margarine,
softened

1 egg

Preheat oven to 375°. In a large mixing bowl, pour brown sugar from top of jar. Add butter and mix at high speed until lightened in texture. Add egg and remaining contents of jar and beat at low speed until well combined. Drop dough by teaspoonfuls onto a lightly greased baking sheet. Bake for 8 to 10 minutes.

Coconut Macadamia Cookies

1 jar Coconut Macadamia
Cookie Mix

¾ C. butter or margarine,
softened

1 egg

Preheat oven to 375°. In a large mixing bowl, pour brown sugar from top of jar. Add butter and mix at high speed until lightened in texture. Add egg and remaining contents of jar and beat at low speed until well combined. Drop dough by teaspoonfuls onto a lightly greased baking sheet. Bake for 8 to 10 minutes.

Coconut Macadamia Cookies

1 jar Coconut
Macadamia
Cookie Mix

¾ C. butter or
margarine, softened

1 egg

Preheat oven to 375°. In a large mixing bowl, pour brown sugar from top of jar. Add butter and mix at high speed until lightened in texture. Add egg and remaining contents of jar and beat at low speed until well combined. Drop dough by teaspoonfuls onto a lightly greased baking sheet. Bake for 8 to 10 minutes.

Peanut Butter Chocolate Chip Cookie Mix

1 C. milk chocolate chips
½ C. quick oats
1½ C. all-purpose flour
¼ tsp. salt
1¼ tsp. baking soda
¼ tsp. baking powder
⅔ C. dark brown sugar
⅔ C. sugar

In a 1-quart container of your choice, layer the above ingredients in order given. Pack each layer into the container before adding the next ingredient.

Securely close container and, if desired, decorate with fabric, ribbon or raffia. Cut out a gift tag with the recipient's directions from the following pages. Simply personalize the tag and attach to your container.

Peanut Butter Chocolate Chip Cookies

1 jar Peanut Butter Chocolate Chip Cookie Mix
⅓ C. butter or margarine, softened
⅓ C. creamy or crunchy peanut butter
1 egg
½ tsp. vanilla

Preheat oven to 375°. In a large mixing bowl, pour sugar and brown sugar from top of jar. Add butter and peanut butter and mix at high speed until light in texture. Add egg and vanilla and beat at medium speed for 1 to 2 minutes. Add remaining contents of jar and beat at low speed until well combined. Drop dough by teaspoonfuls onto a lightly greased baking sheet. Bake for 8 to 10 minutes.

Peanut Butter Chocolate Chip Cookies

1 jar Peanut Butter Chocolate Chip Cookie Mix
⅓ C. butter or margarine, softened
⅓ C. creamy or crunchy peanut butter
1 egg
½ tsp. vanilla

Preheat oven to 375°. In a large mixing bowl, pour sugar and brown sugar from top of jar. Add butter and peanut butter and mix at high speed until light in texture. Add egg and vanilla and beat at medium speed for 1 to 2 minutes. Add remaining contents of jar and beat at low speed until well combined. Drop dough by teaspoonfuls onto a lightly greased baking sheet. Bake for 8 to 10 minutes.

For a quality black and white reproduction, photocopy the above tag. Any of the color tags may also be photocopied for additional gifts.

Peanut Butter Chocolate Chip Cookies

1 jar Peanut Butter
    Chocolate Chip
    Cookie Mix
⅓ C. butter or
    margarine, softened
⅓ C. creamy or
    crunchy peanut butter
1 egg
½ tsp. vanilla

Preheat oven to 375°. In a large mixing bowl, pour sugar and brown sugar from top of jar. Add butter and peanut butter and mix at high speed until light in texture. Add egg and vanilla and beat at medium speed for 1 to 2 minutes. Add remaining contents of jar and beat at low speed until well combined. Drop dough by teaspoonfuls onto a lightly greased baking sheet. Bake for 8 to 10 minutes.

Peanut Butter Chocolate Chip Cookies

1 jar Peanut Butter
    Chocolate Chip
    Cookie Mix
⅓ C. butter or
    margarine, softened
⅓ C. creamy or
    crunchy peanut butter
1 egg
½ tsp. vanilla

Preheat oven to 375°. In a large mixing bowl, pour sugar and brown sugar from top of jar. Add butter and peanut butter and mix at high speed until light in texture. Add egg and vanilla and beat at medium speed for 1 to 2 minutes. Add remaining contents of jar and beat at low speed until well combined. Drop dough by teaspoonfuls onto a lightly greased baking sheet. Bake for 8 to 10 minutes.

Peanut Butter Chocolate Chip Cookies

1 jar Peanut Butter
    Chocolate Chip
    Cookie Mix
⅓ C. butter or
    margarine, softened
⅓ C. creamy or
    crunchy peanut butter
1 egg
½ tsp. vanilla

Preheat oven to 375°. In a large mixing bowl, pour sugar and brown sugar from top of jar. Add butter and peanut butter and mix at high speed until light in texture. Add egg and vanilla and beat at medium speed for 1 to 2 minutes. Add remaining contents of jar and beat at low speed until well combined. Drop dough by teaspoonfuls onto a lightly greased baking sheet. Bake for 8 to 10 minutes.

Peanut Butter Chocolate Chip Cookies

1 jar Peanut Butter
    Chocolate Chip
    Cookie Mix
⅓ C. butter or
    margarine, softened
⅓ C. creamy or
    crunchy peanut butter
1 egg
½ tsp. vanilla

Preheat oven to 375°. In a large mixing bowl, pour sugar and brown sugar from top of jar. Add butter and peanut butter and mix at high speed until light in texture. Add egg and vanilla and beat at medium speed for 1 to 2 minutes. Add remaining contents of jar and beat at low speed until well combined. Drop dough by teaspoonfuls onto a lightly greased baking sheet. Bake for 8 to 10 minutes.

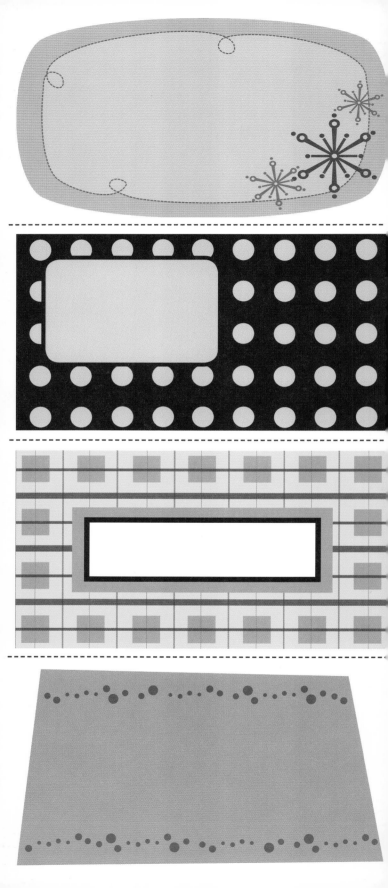

Applesauce Cookie Mix

¾ C. old-fashioned rolled oats
½ C. golden raisins
1 tsp. ground cinnamon
½ tsp. ground nutmeg
1 tsp. instant coffee mix
½ tsp. baking soda
½ tsp. salt
1¾ C. all-purpose flour
1 C. brown sugar

In a 1-quart container of your choice, layer the above ingredients in order given. Pack each layer into the container before adding the next ingredient.

Securely close container and, if desired, decorate with fabric, ribbon or raffia. Cut out a gift tag with the recipient's directions from the following pages. Simply personalize the tag and attach to your container.

Applesauce Cookies

1 jar Applesauce Cookie Mix
½ C. shortening
1 egg
½ C. applesauce

Preheat oven to 375°. In a large mixing bowl, pour brown sugar from top of jar. Add shortening and mix at high speed until light in texture. Add egg and applesauce and beat at high speed for 1 to 2 minutes. Add remaining contents of jar and beat at low speed just until combined. Drop dough by teaspoonfuls onto a lightly greased baking sheet. Bake for 8 to 10 minutes.

Applesauce Cookies

1 jar Applesauce
  Cookie Mix
½ C. shortening
1 egg
½ C. applesauce

Preheat oven to 375°. In a large mixing bowl, pour brown sugar from top of jar. Add shortening and mix at high speed until light in texture. Add egg and applesauce and beat at high speed for 1 to 2 minutes. Add remaining contents of jar and beat at low speed just until combined. Drop dough by teaspoonfuls onto a lightly greased baking sheet. Bake for 8 to 10 minutes.

For a quality black and white reproduction, photocopy the above tag. Any of the color tags may also be photocopied for additional gifts.

Applesauce Cookies

1 jar Applesauce
Cookie Mix
½ C. shortening
1 egg
½ C. applesauce

Preheat oven to 375°. In a large mixing bowl, pour brown sugar from top of jar. Add shortening and mix at high speed until light in texture. Add egg and applesauce and beat at high speed for 1 to 2 minutes. Add remaining contents of jar and beat at low speed just until combined. Drop dough by teaspoonfuls onto a lightly greased baking sheet. Bake for 8 to 10 minutes.

Applesauce Cookies

1 jar Applesauce
Cookie Mix
½ C. shortening
1 egg
½ C. applesauce

Preheat oven to 375°. In a large mixing bowl, pour brown sugar from top of jar. Add shortening and mix at high speed until light in texture. Add egg and applesauce and beat at high speed for 1 to 2 minutes. Add remaining contents of jar and beat at low speed just until combined. Drop dough by teaspoonfuls onto a lightly greased baking sheet. Bake for 8 to 10 minutes.

Applesauce Cookies

1 jar Applesauce
Cookie Mix
½ C. shortening
1 egg
½ C. applesauce

Preheat oven to 375°. In a large mixing bowl, pour brown sugar from top of jar. Add shortening and mix at high speed until light in texture. Add egg and applesauce and beat at high speed for 1 to 2 minutes. Add remaining contents of jar and beat at low speed just until combined. Drop dough by teaspoonfuls onto a lightly greased baking sheet. Bake for 8 to 10 minutes.

Applesauce Cookies

1 jar Applesauce
Cookie Mix
½ C. shortening
1 egg
½ C. applesauce

Preheat oven to 375°. In a large mixing bowl, pour brown sugar from top of jar. Add shortening and mix at high speed until light in texture. Add egg and applesauce and beat at high speed for 1 to 2 minutes. Add remaining contents of jar and beat at low speed just until combined. Drop dough by teaspoonfuls onto a lightly greased baking sheet. Bake for 8 to 10 minutes.

Double Fudge Brownie Mix

2 C. sugar
½ C. unsweetened cocoa powder
1 C. all-purpose flour
½ C. chopped pecans
½ C. semi-sweet chocolate chips

Layer the ingredients in the order given into a 1-quart container of your choice. After adding the unsweetened cocoa powder, but before adding the flour, clean the inside of the jar with a paper towel. Pack each layer into the container before adding the next ingredient.

Securely close container and, if desired, decorate with fabric, ribbon or raffia. Cut out a gift tag with the recipient's directions from the following pages. Simply personalize the tag and attach to your container

Double Fudge Brownies

1 C. butter or margarine, softened
4 eggs
1 jar Double Fudge Brownie Mix

Preheat oven to 325°. In a large bowl, cream the butter. Add the eggs, one at a time, beating well after each egg. Add the Double Fudge Brownie Mix and continue to beat the mixture until smooth. Spread the batter into a greased 9 x 13″ baking pan. Bake for 40 to 50 minutes. Cool before cutting.

Double Fudge Brownies

1 C. butter or
   margarine, softened
4 eggs
1 jar Double Fudge
   Brownie Mix

Preheat oven to 325°. In a large bowl, cream the butter. Add the eggs, one at a time, beating well after each egg. Add the Double Fudge Brownie Mix and continue to beat the mixture until smooth. Spread the batter into a greased 9 x 13″ baking pan. Bake for 40 to 50 minutes. Cool before cutting.

For a quality black and white reproduction, photocopy the above tag. Any of the color tags may also be photocopied for additional gifts.

Double Fudge Brownies

1 C. butter or
margarine, softened
4 eggs
1 jar Double Fudge
Brownie Mix

Preheat oven to 325°. In a large bowl, cream the butter. Add the eggs, one at a time, beating well after each egg. Add the Double Fudge Brownie Mix and continue to beat the mixture until smooth. Spread the batter into a greased 9 x 13″ baking pan. Bake for 40 to 50 minutes. Cool before cutting.

Double Fudge Brownies

1 C. butter or
margarine, softened
4 eggs
1 jar Double Fudge
Brownie Mix

Preheat oven to 325°. In a large bowl, cream the butter. Add the eggs, one at a time, beating well after each egg. Add the Double Fudge Brownie Mix and continue to beat the mixture until smooth. Spread the batter into a greased 9 x 13″ baking pan. Bake for 40 to 50 minutes. Cool before cutting.

Double Fudge Brownies

1 C. butter or
margarine, softened
4 eggs
1 jar Double Fudge
Brownie Mix

Preheat oven to 325°. In a large bowl, cream the butter. Add the eggs, one at a time, beating well after each egg. Add the Double Fudge Brownie Mix and continue to beat the mixture until smooth. Spread the batter into a greased 9 x 13″ baking pan. Bake for 40 to 50 minutes. Cool before cutting.

Double Fudge Brownies

1 C. butter or
margarine, softened
4 eggs
1 jar Double Fudge
Brownie Mix

Preheat oven to 325°. In a large bowl, cream the butter. Add the eggs, one at a time, beating well after each egg. Add the Double Fudge Brownie Mix and continue to beat the mixture until smooth. Spread the batter into a greased 9 x 13″ baking pan. Bake for 40 to 50 minutes. Cool before cutting.

Butterscotch Oatmeal Cookie Mix

½ C. all-purpose flour
⅓ C. quick oats
1 C. butterscotch chips
1 C. quick oats
½ C. all-purpose flour
½ tsp. baking soda
½ tsp. baking powder
¼ tsp. salt
1 C. dark brown sugar

In a 1-quart container of your choice, layer the above ingredients in order given. Pack each layer into the container before adding the next ingredient.

Securely close container and, if desired, decorate with fabric, ribbon or raffia. Cut out a gift tag with the recipient's directions from the following pages. Simply personalize the tag and attach to your container.

Butterscotch Oatmeal Cookies

1 jar Butterscotch Oatmeal Cookie Mix
½ C. plus 2 T. butter or margarine, softened
1½ tsp. vanilla
1 egg

Preheat oven to 375°. In a large mixing bowl, pour brown sugar from top of jar. Add butter and mix at high speed until lightened in texture. Add vanilla and egg and beat at high speed for 1 to 2 minutes. Add remaining ingredients from jar and beat at low speed until well combined. Drop dough by teaspoonfuls onto a lightly greased baking sheet. Bake for 8 to 10 minutes.

Butterscotch Oatmeal Cookies

1 jar Butterscotch Oatmeal Cookie Mix
½ C. plus 2 T. butter or margarine, softened
1½ tsp. vanilla
1 egg

Preheat oven to 375°. In a large mixing bowl, pour brown sugar from top of jar. Add butter and mix at high speed until lightened in texture. Add vanilla and egg and beat at high speed for 1 to 2 minutes. Add remaining ingredients from jar and beat at low speed until well combined. Drop dough by teaspoonfuls onto a lightly greased baking sheet. Bake for 8 to 10 minutes.

For a quality black and white reproduction, photocopy the above tag. Any of the color tags may also be photocopied for additional gifts.

Butterscotch Oatmeal Cookies

1 jar Butterscotch
  Oatmeal Cookie Mix
½ C. plus 2 T. butter or
  margarine, softened
1½ tsp. vanilla
1 egg

Preheat oven to 375°. In a large mixing bowl, pour brown sugar from top of jar. Add butter and mix at high speed until lightened in texture. Add vanilla and egg and beat at high speed for 1 to 2 minutes. Add remaining ingredients from jar and beat at low speed until well combined. Drop dough by teaspoonfuls onto a lightly greased baking sheet. Bake for 8 to 10 minutes.

Butterscotch Oatmeal Cookies

1 jar Butterscotch
  Oatmeal Cookie Mix
½ C. plus 2 T. butter or
  margarine, softened
1½ tsp. vanilla
1 egg

Preheat oven to 375°. In a large mixing bowl, pour brown sugar from top of jar. Add butter and mix at high speed until lightened in texture. Add vanilla and egg and beat at high speed for 1 to 2 minutes. Add remaining ingredients from jar and beat at low speed until well combined. Drop dough by teaspoonfuls onto a lightly greased baking sheet. Bake for 8 to 10 minutes.

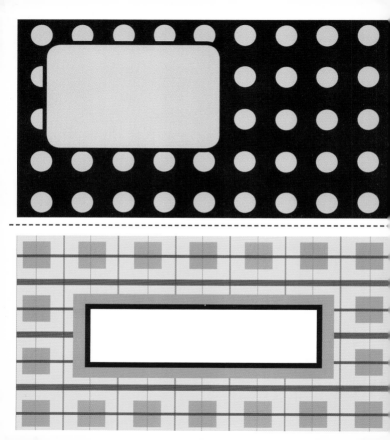

Dutch Cookie Mix

⅔ C. quick oats
¼ C. shredded coconut
½ C. chopped walnuts or pecans
½ C. corn flakes or wheat flakes cereal
½ tsp. baking soda
¾ tsp. baking powder
1 C. all-purpose flour
⅓ C. brown sugar
⅔ C. sugar

In a 1-quart container of your choice, layer the above ingredients in order given. Pack each layer into the container before adding the next ingredient.

Securely close container and, if desired, decorate with fabric, ribbon or raffia. Cut out a gift tag with the recipient's directions from the following pages. Simply personalize the tag and attach to your container.

Dutch Cookies

1 jar Dutch Cookie Mix
½ C. shortening
2 T. butter or margarine, softened
1 egg

Preheat oven to 375°. In a large mixing bowl, pour sugar and brown sugar from top of jar. Add shortening and butter and mix at high speed until light in texture. Add egg and beat at high speed for 1 to 2 minutes. Add remaining contents of jar and beat at low speed until well combined. Drop dough by teaspoonfuls onto a lightly greased baking sheet. Bake for 8 to 10 minutes.

Dutch Cookies

1 jar Dutch Cookie Mix
½ C. shortening
2 T. butter or margarine, softened
1 egg

Preheat oven to 375°. In a large mixing bowl, pour sugar and brown sugar from top of jar. Add shortening and butter and mix at high speed until light in texture. Add egg and beat at high speed for 1 to 2 minutes. Add remaining contents of jar and beat at low speed until well combined. Drop dough by teaspoonfuls onto a lightly greased baking sheet. Bake for 8 to 10 minutes.

For a quality black and white reproduction, photocopy the above tag. Any of the color tags may also be photocopied for additional gifts.

Dutch Cookies

1 jar Dutch Cookie Mix
½ C. shortening
2 T. butter or margarine,
  softened
1 egg

Preheat oven to 375°. In a large mixing bowl, pour sugar and brown sugar from top of jar. Add shortening and butter and mix at high speed until light in texture. Add egg and beat at high speed for 1 to 2 minutes. Add remaining contents of jar and beat at low speed until well combined. Drop dough by teaspoonfuls onto a lightly greased baking sheet. Bake for 8 to 10 minutes.

Dutch Cookies

1 jar Dutch Cookie Mix
½ C. shortening
2 T. butter or margarine,
  softened
1 egg

Preheat oven to 375°. In a large mixing bowl, pour sugar and brown sugar from top of jar. Add shortening and butter and mix at high speed until light in texture. Add egg and beat at high speed for 1 to 2 minutes. Add remaining contents of jar and beat at low speed until well combined. Drop dough by teaspoonfuls onto a lightly greased baking sheet. Bake for 8 to 10 minutes.

Dutch Cookies

1 jar Dutch Cookie Mix
½ C. shortening
2 T. butter or margarine,
  softened
1 egg

Preheat oven to 375°. In a large mixing bowl, pour sugar and brown sugar from top of jar. Add shortening and butter and mix at high speed until light in texture. Add egg and beat at high speed for 1 to 2 minutes. Add remaining contents of jar and beat at low speed until well combined. Drop dough by teaspoonfuls onto a lightly greased baking sheet. Bake for 8 to 10 minutes.

Dutch Cookies

1 jar Dutch Cookie Mix
½ C. shortening
2 T. butter or margarine,
  softened
1 egg

Preheat oven to 375°. In a large mixing bowl, pour sugar and brown sugar from top of jar. Add shortening and butter and mix at high speed until light in texture. Add egg and beat at high speed for 1 to 2 minutes. Add remaining contents of jar and beat at low speed until well combined. Drop dough by teaspoonfuls onto a lightly greased baking sheet. Bake for 8 to 10 minutes.

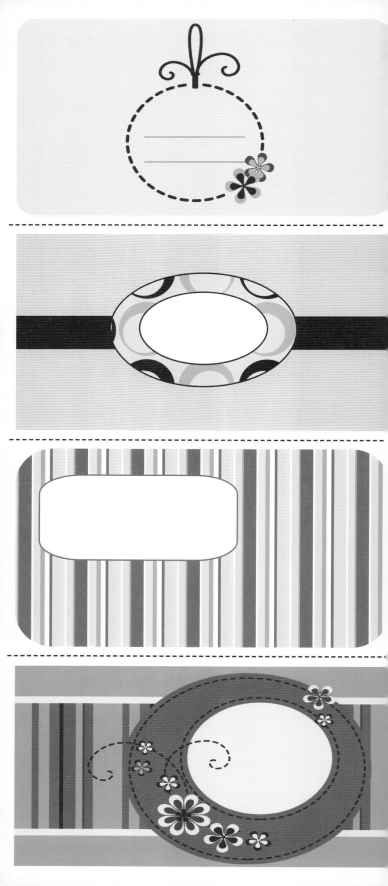

Cinnamon Applesauce Loaf Mix

¾ C. sugar
¾ C. chopped pecans or raisins
½ C. brown sugar
2 tsp. baking powder
1 tsp. baking soda
1 tsp. ground cinnamon
¼ tsp. salt
2¼ C. all-purpose flour

In a 1-quart container of your choice, layer
the above ingredients in order given. Pack
each layer into the container before adding
the next ingredient.

Securely close container and, if desired, decorate
with fabric, ribbon or raffia. Cut out a gift
tag with the recipient's directions from the
following pages. Simply personalize the tag
and attach to your container.

Cinnamon Applesauce Loaf

2 eggs
½ tsp. vanilla
¾ C. vegetable oil
1 C. applesauce
1 jar Cinnamon Applesauce Loaf Mix

Preheat oven to 350°. In a large bowl, combine eggs, vanilla and vegetable oil. Stir until well blended. Add applesauce and contents of jar; mix well. Pour batter into a lightly greased 8-cup loaf pan. Bake for 55 to 60 minutes.

Cinnamon Applesauce Loaf

2 eggs
½ tsp. vanilla
¾ C. vegetable oil
1 C. applesauce
1 jar Cinnamon Applesauce Loaf Mix

Preheat oven to 350°. In a large bowl, combine eggs, vanilla and vegetable oil. Stir until well blended. Add applesauce and contents of jar; mix well. Pour batter into a lightly greased 8-cup loaf pan. Bake for 55 to 60 minutes.

For a quality black and white reproduction, photocopy the above tag. Any of the color tags may also be photocopied for additional gifts.

Cinnamon Applesauce Loaf

2 eggs
½ tsp. vanilla
¾ C. vegetable oil
1 C. applesauce
1 jar Cinnamon
  Applesauce
  Loaf Mix

Preheat oven to 350°. In a large bowl, combine eggs, vanilla and vegetable oil. Stir until well blended. Add applesauce and contents of jar; mix well. Pour batter into a lightly greased 8-cup loaf pan. Bake for 55 to 60 minutes.

Cinnamon Applesauce Loaf

2 eggs
½ tsp. vanilla
¾ C. vegetable oil
1 C. applesauce
1 jar Cinnamon
  Applesauce Loaf Mix

Preheat oven to 350°. In a large bowl, combine eggs, vanilla and vegetable oil. Stir until well blended. Add applesauce and contents of jar; mix well. Pour batter into a lightly greased 8-cup loaf pan. Bake for 55 to 60 minutes.

Cinnamon Applesauce Loaf

2 eggs
½ tsp. vanilla
¾ C. vegetable oil
1 C. applesauce
1 jar Cinnamon
  Applesauce Loaf Mix

Preheat oven to 350°. In a large bowl, combine eggs, vanilla and vegetable oil. Stir until well blended. Add applesauce and contents of jar; mix well. Pour batter into a lightly greased 8-cup loaf pan. Bake for 55 to 60 minutes.

Cinnamon Applesauce Loaf

2 eggs
½ tsp. vanilla
¾ C. vegetable oil
1 C. applesauce
1 jar Cinnamon
  Applesauce Loaf Mix

Preheat oven to 350°. In a large bowl, combine eggs, vanilla and vegetable oil. Stir until well blended. Add applesauce and contents of jar; mix well. Pour batter into a lightly greased 8-cup loaf pan. Bake for 55 to 60 minutes.

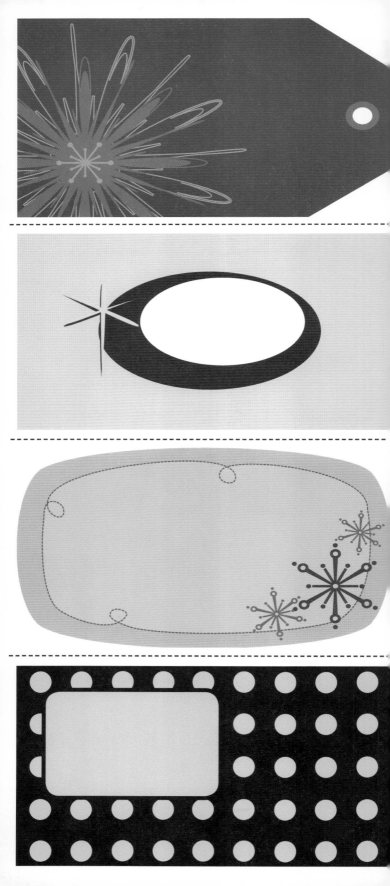

Chocolate M&M Cookie Mix

1½ C. all-purpose flour
1 tsp. baking soda
½ C. dry instant chocolate pudding mix
1⅓ C. M&M's
½ C. brown sugar
⅓ C. sugar

In a 1-quart container of your choice, layer the above ingredients in order given. Pack each layer into the container before adding the next ingredient.

Securely close container and, if desired, decorate with fabric, ribbon or raffia. Cut out a gift tag with the recipient's directions from the following pages. Simply personalize the tag and attach to your container.

Chocolate M&M Cookies

1 jar Chocolate M&M Cookie Mix
⅔ C. butter or margarine, softened
1 tsp. vanilla
2 eggs

Preheat oven to 375°. In a large mixing bowl, pour sugar and brown sugar from top of jar. Add butter and mix at high speed until light in texture. Add vanilla and eggs and beat at high speed for 1 minute. Add remaining ingredients from jar and mix until just combined. Drop dough by teaspoonfuls onto a lightly greased baking sheet. Bake for 8 to 10 minutes.

Chocolate M&M Cookies

1 jar Chocolate M&M Cookie Mix
⅔ C. butter or margarine, softened
1 tsp. vanilla
2 eggs

Preheat oven to 375°. In a large mixing bowl, pour sugar and brown sugar from top of jar. Add butter and mix at high speed until light in texture. Add vanilla and eggs and beat at high speed for 1 minute. Add remaining ingredients from jar and mix until just combined. Drop dough by teaspoonfuls onto a lightly greased baking sheet. Bake for 8 to 10 minutes.

For a quality black and white reproduction, photocopy the above tag. Any of the color tags may also be photocopied for additional gifts.

Chocolate M&M Cookies

1 jar Chocolate M&M
Cookie Mix

⅔ C. butter or
margarine, softened

1 tsp. vanilla

2 eggs

Preheat oven to 375°. In a large mixing bowl,
pour sugar and brown sugar from top of jar.
Add butter and mix at high speed until light
in texture. Add vanilla and eggs and beat
at high speed for 1 minute. Add remaining
ingredients from jar and mix until just
combined. Drop dough by teaspoonfuls
onto a lightly greased baking sheet. Bake
for 8 to 10 minutes.

Chocolate M&M Cookies

1 jar Chocolate M&M
Cookie Mix

⅔ C. butter or
margarine, softened

1 tsp. vanilla

2 eggs

Preheat oven to 375°. In a large mixing bowl, pour
sugar and brown sugar from top of jar. Add butter
and mix at high speed until light in texture. Add
vanilla and eggs and beat at high speed for 1 minute.
Add remaining ingredients from jar and mix until just
combined. Drop dough by teaspoonfuls onto a lightly
greased baking sheet. Bake for 8 to 10 minutes.

Chocolate M&M Cookies

1 jar Chocolate M&M
Cookie Mix

⅔ C. butter or
margarine, softened

1 tsp. vanilla

2 eggs

Preheat oven to 375°. In a large mixing bowl,
pour sugar and brown sugar from top of jar.
Add butter and mix at high speed until light in
texture. Add vanilla and eggs and beat at high
speed for 1 minute. Add remaining ingredients
from jar and mix until just combined. Drop
dough by teaspoonfuls onto a lightly greased
baking sheet. Bake for 8 to 10 minutes.

Chocolate M&M Cookies

1 jar Chocolate M&M
Cookie Mix

⅔ C. butter or
margarine, softened

1 tsp. vanilla

2 eggs

Preheat oven to 375°. In a large mixing bowl, pour
sugar and brown sugar from top of jar. Add butter
and mix at high speed until light in texture. Add
vanilla and eggs and beat at high speed for
1 minute. Add remaining ingredients from jar
and mix until just combined. Drop dough by
teaspoonfuls onto a lightly greased baking sheet.
Bake for 8 to 10 minutes.

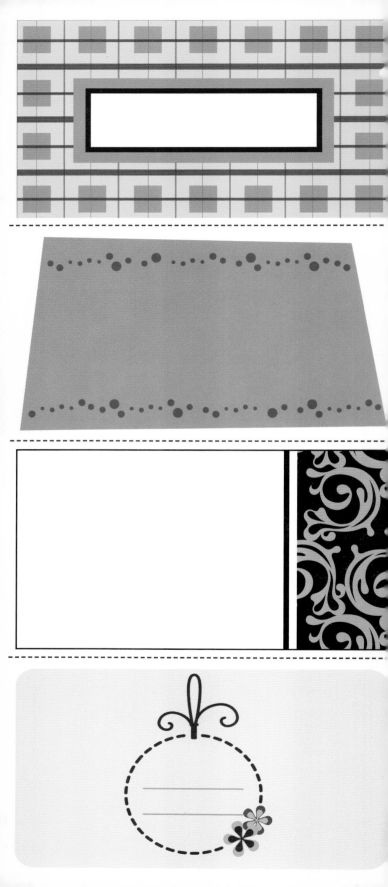

Index

Coordinate with Holidays!

• Color white sugar or coconut by placing the sugar or coconut along with a few drops of food coloring in a container with a tight lid. Shake vigorously. Adjust with additional food coloring if color is too light. If sugar clumps, use a sifter to separate. Spread on a paper plate or wax paper to dry. Dry completely before adding to jar mix.

• Consider substituting holiday theme M&M's for regular and substitute dried cherries or cranberries in place of raisins.

Collect All Four!

Create yummy gifts from your kitchen!